How Do Engineers Solve Problems?

HOUGHTON MIFFLIN HARCOURT

PHOTOGRAPHY CREDITS: 3 (b) ©JCVSTOCK-ES\Fotolia; 4 (b) Comstock/Getty Images; 8 (t) Stockbyte/Getty Images; 9 (l) ©JGI/Jamie Grill/Getty Images; 9 (r) Image100/Alamy; 10 (t) Comstock / Getty Images; 10 (bl) ©Corbis; 10 (r) ©Reven T.C. Wurman/Alamy Images; 10 (tr) ©Scanrail/Fotolia; 10 (cr) Jupiterimages/Getty Images

Copyright © by Houghton Mifflin Harcourt Publishing Company

All rights reserved. No part of this work may be reproduced or transmitted in any form or by any means, electronic or mechanical, including photocopying or recording, or by any information storage and retrieval system, without the prior written permission of the copyright owner unless such copying is expressly permitted by federal copyright law. Requests for permission to make copies of any part of the work should be addressed to Houghton Mifflin Harcourt Publishing Company, Attn: Contracts, Copyrights, and Licensing, 9400 Southpark Center Loop, Orlando, Florida 32819-8647.

If you have received these materials as examination copies free of charge, Houghton Mifflin Harcourt Publishing Company retains title to the materials and they may not be resold. Resale of examination copies is strictly prohibited.

Possession of this publication in print format does not entitle users to convert this publication, or any portion of it, into electronic format.

Printed in Mexico

ISBN: 978-0-544-07209-1

2 3 4 5 6 7 8 9 10 0908 21 20 19 18 17 16 15 14 13

4500456309   A B C D E F G

Be an Active Reader!

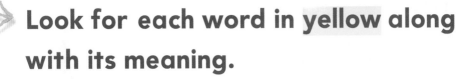 Look for each word in yellow along with its meaning.

engineer	human-made
design process	natural
materials	

 <u>Underlined</u> sentences answer these questions.

What does an engineer do?

What is the design process?

How can we solve a problem?

What are objects made of?

How can we classify materials?

What does an engineer do?

An engineer finds answers to problems. Engineers make plans. These plans show how to make things.

Engineers plan how to build planes.

What is the design process?

The design process is a set of steps.

1. Find a Problem
2. Plan and Build
3. Test and Improve
4. Redesign
5. Communicate

a building plan

How can you solve this problem?

A holder solves the problem.

Here is a problem. You do not have a place for your pencils and markers. You build something. It holds pencils and markers.

How can you fix this problem?

Make a plan.

How can we solve a problem?

1. Find a Problem: A plant gets too much sun.

2. Plan and Build: Draw pictures. Make a plant shade.

3. Test and Improve: The plant shade falls down. Make it smaller.

4. <u>Redesign</u>: Build it smaller.
5. <u>Communicate</u>: Tell a friend.

Sharing your plan helps a friend.

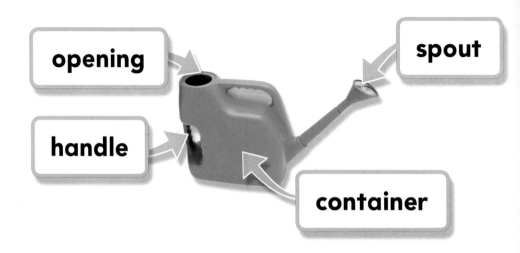

opening

spout

handle

container

What are objects made of?

An object has parts. The parts work together.

Objects are made of materials. The watering can is made of a material. It might be metal. It might be something else.

Wool comes from sheep.

People make bottles and cans.

Human-made materials are made by people. Natural materials are found in nature.

How can we classify materials?

Look at the objects. Name each one. What is each object made of? Is it made of natural materials? Is it made of human-made materials? Is it made of both?

Draw the chart below on a sheet of paper. Sort the objects from page 10. Draw each object on the chart.

Sort the Objects

Natural	Human-made	Both

Draw and Label

Draw a picture of something natural. Draw a picture of something human-made. Label each picture.

Make a Plan

Work with a partner. Think of a problem. Make a plan. Write your plan on paper. Draw a picture of your design. Test it. Make it better. Share it.